THE DAILY LEARNER

BOOK 1

DAILY WEALTH

ALSO BY PARTH SAWHNEY

The Daily Apple

Thriving in the New Normal

The Way of the Karma Yogi

Elevation

The Detachment Manifesto

Becoming a Karma Yogi

DAILY WEALTH

---

21 Life-Changing Meditations on Personal Finance Management and Investing

PARTH SAWHNEY

Published by Parth Sawhney

DAILY WEALTH

First published in 2021

Printed and bound by Draft2Digital, LLC

Contents

"Rule No. 1: Never lose money. Rule No. 2: Never forget Rule No. 1."
— Warren Buffett

"A wise person should have money in their head, but not in their heart."
— Jonathan Swift

Introduction

First of all, I'm immensely grateful to you for picking this book and equally glad that you decided to take a step forward in your self-education and personal development journey.

This book is an attempt from me to distill the life-changing ideas from the best resources on finances, money management and investing into clear and concise daily meditations. I'm a big believer in doing the actions and behaviors that enhance our success and help us grow on a daily basis. As Jim Rohn aptly said, "Success is nothing more than a few simple disciplines, practiced every day."

In the following pages, I have tried to capture the wisdom with regard to money and wealth in a form that is easy to digest and consume (even if you're not a reader!). It's hard to capture an entire book in a few paragraphs, but every meditation has been crafted to give you the essence and the formula, if you will, introduced by the respective author to make you wealthy. I'm sure your money game will elevate and reach a new higher level in a short time if you put the principles I have mentioned in the following pages into practice.

Wisdom is timeless. The fundamentals to becoming wealthy will never change and financial success and freedom are inevitable when you choose to align your actions with them.

Through this book, my intention for you is to develop a mindset of wealth and abundance over the next 21 days. Success is all about habits, and that's why I've chosen 21 days to get you started with the learning process. If you're serious about making a deep-level change in your psychology and creating a millionaire mindset, I urge to read the meditation once in the morning after you wake up, and once before sleeping at night. To be certain that this habit sticks, I would highly encourage you to keep reading or listening to books, podcasts and other resources to continue your self-education in personal finances management.

As you read the meditations, some patterns will emerge. When internalized, they will guide you in your quest to become a wealthy person. If any meditation piques your interest, feel free to embark further in your self-education journey and read the respective book. At the end of this book, I have gathered all the important takeaways and listed them in the final chapter, *Pithy Insights* for your reference.

Once you are done reading this book, I would be grateful if you pay forward by recommending this to your loved ones. As you will learn in the following pages, cultivating a discipline to give will attract more money, prosperity and abundance in your life.

Last but not the least, keep coming back to this book whenever you get a chance. Repetition is the mother of skill. I'll be honored if this book ends up becoming a part of your personal library and your quick go-to guide for re-calibrating to the wealth mindset as you go ahead in your journey.

I hope you enjoy reading this book as much as I have enjoyed writing it.

Wishing you excellence and everlasting success!

Parth Sawhney

Day 1: Striving for Mastery

"Life isn't about waiting for the storm to pass; it's about learning to dance in the rain. It's about removing the fear in this area of your life so you can focus on what matters most."
— Anthony Robbins, *Money: Master the Game*

Are you working hard for money or is the money working hard for you? In order to achieve financial freedom, we need to take a step-by-step approach. Money can't buy us happiness but it can help us in living the life that we truly want to live and have our desired experiences. We need to become masters of money. We have to get ourselves in a position to instruct it where to go, and not the other way around.

The best way is to educate ourselves so that we make the right investments. We need to take calculated risks and protect the downside so that we don't sabotage our financial security. An important thing is to make investments with trustworthy people. As the money keeps on compounding, eventually we can get a consistent flow of income and live a life without ever working again. Once our basic needs are fulfilled, we can spend the rest of our money to enhance the quality of our lives and others'.

Dedication and discipline will lead us to financial freedom. We have to structure our lives in such a way so that we can save money for our future selves. Identify all the unnecessary expenses you have, and redirect that money towards saving and investments. The process will be slow. We have to keep believing in it and ourselves, as we face the financial storms. We need to be consistent without any shred of doubt or fear and have total faith that things are working out for us.

Day 2: Baby Steps

"Winning at money is 80 percent behavior and 20 percent head knowledge. What to do isn't the problem; doing it is. Most of us know what to do, but we just don't do it. If I can control the guy in the mirror, I can be skinny and rich."

— Dave Ramsey, *The Total Money Makeover: Classic Edition*

How do you eat an elephant? One bite at a time. And that's exactly how we can make sure we have financial security and eventually financial freedom.

Debt helps us fulfill our current desires but it robs us of our happiness in the future. When we use credit cards, we create the illusion that we have unlimited money and we can spend it freely without any inhibitions. But the truth is that they are like leeches that cling to us and keep sucking the money out of our bank accounts without us noticing. We think buying stuff will make us happy and our lifestyle demands it. We need to fit in with the people around us. But spending carelessly is being childish and it can be detrimental to our mental and financial health.

As Dave Ramsey says, financial success is 80% behavior and 20% head knowledge, it is important that we become aware of our reckless behaviors and keep them in check. Once we do that, we'll be able to keep our finances intact.

Today, get started with the seven baby steps to get you on the path to financial security. Stop worrying about keeping up with the Joneses and make your own financial success your priority. It's never too late to start.

Day 3: Aim for the Riches

"Whatever may be said in praise of poverty, the fact remains that it is not possible to live a really complete or successful life unless one is rich. "
— Wallace D. Wattles, *The Science of Getting Rich*

When we focus on a particular idea or thought, the formless Substance makes sure that it comes into material expression. This concurs with what the great inventor Thomas Edison once said: "Ideas come from space." We need to be able to see things first before they manifest in the physical reality. This can happen by practicing visualization on a repetitive basis.

If you see around, the way of nature is growth and expansion. Hence, it is natural for us to want more. The desire to be wealthy is a sign of progress and growth. It's a way for us to reach our truest expression and unlock our highest potential. Also, money helps us to have experiences that fascinate us and bring us joy. Becoming rich is the best way to make a difference in the world and inspire others.

We need money to educate ourselves by buying books and

hence fulfilling our intellectual potential. We have to make the most of our natural talents and abilities so that we can add value to other people's lives. If our thoughts contradict this process, then we go against the natural flow of the Universe. When we get into a mindset of competition, it deteriorates our creative nature. Never complain about lack and poverty, and never make it a focus of your attention.

The Universe is abundant and we have an endless flow of the riches that we want. And our gratitude towards things that we already have fuels this flow of abundance.

Day 4: Get Your Thoughts Dialed In

"Wishing will not bring riches. But desiring riches with a state of mind that becomes an obsession, then planning definite ways and means to acquire riches, and backing those plans with persistence which does not recognize failure, will bring riches."
— Napoleon Hill, *Think and Grow Rich*

Burning desire — that is what will take us from where we are to where we want to be. Rejections, frustrations, and failures will always come your way. But it is your attitude that'll dictate your success. Determine the precise amount of money that you want to make and start designing a road map that'll take you there. Let your imagination soar! Understand what it'll take from you to arrive at your desired destination.

Even though the current situation may seem dire, have an unwavering faith in yourself that you are destined to be wealthy and successful. We can develop this faith in ourselves through auto-suggestion. Through positive self-talk, we can persuade ourselves to believe that our thoughts can be transformed into reality and our dreams can come true. Our subconscious mind holds key to this and success becomes easier when we have it on our side.

If our desire is to become wealthy, we need to become persistent and be ready to encounter all troubles and obstacles we may face in our journey. We need to surround ourselves with like-minded people that are smart and support our vision.

Another important prerequisite for becoming rich and successful in the true sense is to become a lifelong learner. By committing to self-education, we become self-aware. We begin understanding our strengths and weaknesses and unlock our true potential.

Day 5: Simplify

"The easiest way to manage your money is to take it one step at a time—and not worry about being perfect."
— Ramit Sethi, *I Will Teach You To Be Rich*

Managing our finances can be effortless if we know the inner workings of the financial world and automate the flow of our money. Know where your money is spending its time and choose your bank accounts wisely. If you have credit card debt, now is the time to get rid of it with a disciplined approach.

When you prepare your budget, make sure you have a plan to spend consciously. This can be done by spending on things that you really want to and reducing the expenses in the categories that are not important to you. Changing behaviors can take some time so be patient and set yourself mini-goals. Tiny wins will keep you on track and help you develop consistency.

The best way to get the money working for you is by investing. Setting up a retirement account is a good place to start. The amount that you save and invest every month doesn't matter, but it's the habit formation that will change your game. Automation is a lifesaver! Have a fixed percentage of your savings and investments automatically withdrawn from your account. Automating your recurring expenses and bill payments will also free up a lot of your headspace.

Taking charge and simplifying your approach will eliminate your anxieties and worries about money. When you're done, all you have to do is sit back, relax and watch it grow!

Day 6: Becoming a Millionaire

"Money should never change one's values… Making money is only a report card. It's a way to tell how you're doing."
— Thomas J. Stanley, *The Millionaire Next Door*

On the contrary to the popular belief, a millionaire life is a modest life. Despite the stereotype of having glamor, glitz and flashy gadgets, in reality, millionaires are huge savers and live an intentional life. They prefer their money in bank accounts and investments, rather than showing it off.

Millionaires direct their funds to improving their business and seeking better investment and financial advice, rather than on irrelevant expenses. Even though they are frugal, they never compromise on the health and well-being of themselves and their loved ones.

We need to give more emphasis to financial independence than luxury. A prerequisite to spending smartly is to plan smartly. The secret formula to becoming a millionaire is to plan and structure your expenses and spend less than what you make. If you start thinking long-term and have a great plan in place, you too can become a millionaire!

Day 7: Reprogram Your Mind

"You have to believe that you are the one who creates your success, that you are the one who creates your mediocrity, and that you are the one creating your struggles around money and success. Consciously or unconsciously, it's still you."
— T. Harv Eker, *Secrets of the Millionaire Mind*

Our money mindset is dictated by the influences that we've had in our childhood. Our minds are like computers, and we get programmed by the beliefs and thoughts of the people around us as we grow up. We study our parents' aberrant behaviors and their thinking gets downloaded in our brains. We start nurturing the same beliefs that limit us from making money. We need to become aware of such faulty thinking patterns and unlearn them so that we can start building new healthy beliefs around money.

Analyze your finances and self-examine how your behavior is dictating your bank account balance. If it doesn't look good and if it's not the amount that you want to see, then it's time to flip the switch inside and cultivate the millionaire mind.

Reading books and accruing knowledge is not enough. You need to reprogram your brain. If you want to become a millionaire, you need to be in the driver's seat. And you have to constantly course-correct yourself so that you're on the path to accumulating wealth. There is no harm in liking money and removing obstacles so that it flows to us easily. Instead of harboring envy and resentment towards wealthy people, you need to admire them and get inspired. Unless you do this, you will never become rich in the true sense.

It's time to start having an unwavering faith in yourself and your capabilities. It's time to develop an unconditional commitment to becoming rich.

Day 8: Focus On Building Assets

"The love of money is the root of all evil.
The lack of money is the root of all evil."
— Robert T. Kiyosaki, *Rich Dad, Poor Dad*

"Get good grades and secure a high-paying job" is a false societal mantra to become wealthy. Getting involved in the rat race actually minimizes our chances of becoming wealthy.

Unfortunately, a lot of us have no training in financial well-being. When it comes to making money, formal education doesn't take us too far. As Jim Rohn said, "Formal education will make you a living; self-education will make you a fortune." We need to educate ourselves and gain financial intelligence. Invest in yourself and your education. Billionaire Warren Buffett echoes this truth in his famous quote: "The most important investment you can make is in yourself." We need to start acquiring skills that will elevate our income and help us in building wealth.

When it comes to money, emotions can sway us from making the right choices. That's when financial knowledge helps us in making the correct decisions when we are faced with negative emotions like fear and greed. We need to learn to take risks and start investing our money in stocks and bonds instead of just keeping them stagnated in our bank accounts. Not taking any risks can prove to be a bigger risk for us. Other investments such as real estate are also available to us.

Lastly, we need to be able to distinguish between assets and liabilities. It's wise for us to invest only in assets that put more money in our pocket and avoid liabilities that do the exact opposite. This will lead us to become financially independent in the true sense.

Day 9: Get In the Fastlane

"Money is like a mischievous cat; if you chase it around the neighborhood, it eludes you. It hides up a tree, behind the rose bush, or in the garden. However, if you ignore it and focus on what attracts the cat, it comes to you and sits in your lap."
— M.J. DeMarco, *The Millionaire Fastlane*

The conventional path to wealth is not practical. There's always a cap on how much we can earn in our day jobs and we hit the glass ceiling sooner or later. Rather than waiting for retirement to enjoy your life, retire young! It's wise to do the things that you've always wished for when you have the vitality and energy.

To become wealthy we need to come up with a business or product that is self-sustaining so that even when we're not working it still generates consistent revenue. We are conditioned with the mindset of being a consumer but to become wealthy we need to cultivate the mindset of a producer. We need to know how we can link our passions with the current demands of the customers, and how we can add value to their lives. You don't need a degree from a prestigious university or credentials to become rich. It's all about acquiring the right skills that you need for your business. Isn't it interesting that some of the most successful and wealthy people such as Bill Gates and Mark Zuckerberg never completed their college education?

True wealth is not only about having a positive cash flow, but it involves having the three most essential components: optimum health and fitness, meaningful relationships and the freedom to do things that we really love to do.

Day 10: What's Your Plan?

"The best financial plan has nothing to do with what the markets are doing, nothing to do with what your real estate agent is telling you, nothing to do with the hot stock your brother-in-law told you about. It has everything to do with what's most important to you."
— Carl Richards, *The One-Page Financial Plan*

In order to reach our goals, we need to have a clear understanding of our assets and liabilities. In that way, we get to know our current net worth and a clear picture of where we are right now. Once we have this information, we become better equipped to take the next action steps in our financial journey. Goal-setting is powerful, but we also need to understand that our future is unpredictable. Our goals may change over time, and they're not set in stone. We need to be flexible.

Financial success can become a possibility if you know how to budget wisely. This involves tracking your spending and measure that against your goals and adjust accordingly. Our investments should always be driven to make profits and reach our financial goals.

There is no one-size-fits-all approach to making a financial plan. First, we need to figure out what our needs are and ask ourselves some deep questions: Why is money important for me? What are the goals that I'm trying to achieve? Are these goals in alignment with my core values, and are my current actions congruent with them?

Day 11: Wisdom From Babylon

"Without wisdom, gold is quickly lost by those who have it, but with wisdom, gold can be secured by those who have it not."
— George S. Clason, *The Richest Man in Babylon*

Some people like saving money and are incredibly frugal; some people are spenders and squander all the money that they make. Ancient Babylonian wisdom suggests that we should do the following two things to make money and become wealthy: primarily, we need to live below our means and secondly, we need to save and invest wisely. Our goal should not be to live a luxurious life when we start. When we live below our means, we are able to direct the remainder amount to savings and investments, which end up making us more money in the long run.

Many people spend more than what they earn by accumulating debt. In that way, you're paying more money for your purchases in the form of additional interest amounts. This robs you of your money and its wealth-making potential. But when you save money and direct that money towards investments, you end up getting more money in return. For instance, getting dividends for your investments in stocks and bonds, and getting interest money along with the amount that you lend to someone. Be the lender, not the borrower!

When it comes to investing, we need to do it wisely. This entails investing exclusively in people and organizations that are trustworthy, and not reckless with our money. We need to be content that they have the required knowledge to handle our money in the best possible way. The goal is to let money work tirelessly for you and make you wealthier over time, not the opposite!

Day 12: Become a Deliberate Creator

"When you remember that you get the essence of what you think about—and then you notice what you are getting—you have the keys for Deliberate Creation. "
— Esther Hicks, *Money and the Law of Attraction*

Have you ever wondered why some people work extremely hard all their lives but still never become rich, while others enjoy their riches even though they spend little to no time working?

The truth is becoming wealthy is under your conscious control. You have to become a deliberate creator of the life and financial success you want. You may think that there are some invisible forces that are stopping you from getting the money that you need, but this is not true. If you always choose powerlessness and victimhood, you will never be able to become wealthy.

The *Law of Attraction* brings to you what you focus on. Because money is such an important topic for all of us and we spend a lot of our time focusing our thoughts on it, we must clean up our vibrations and switch to thoughts that reflect abundance and prosperity. This will improve not only your financial life but the ripple effect will improve other aspects of your life as well.

You are meant to live a life that is extraordinary, expansive and enriched with good feeling moments. Today, reclaim your power and commit to changing the frequency of your thoughts from lack to prosperity.

Day 13: Inject Some Love

"Any relationship worth having is worth deepening
by taking regular, loving actions."
— Kate Northrup, *Money: A Love Story*

Managing your money can be a fun and loving process if you choose it to be. In order to get financial freedom, we need to change our relationship with money. When you take care of your finances, you take care of yourself. And hence, it's an act of self-care. You are in a better place when you are in control of your money and have the freedom to choose where you want to direct it.

It is important to pay attention to your money on a consistent basis. Wherever your attention goes, energy flows. Track your daily expenses and educate yourself on ways to save and bring more money into your life every day. Make a monthly plan for your money and be aware of where it is going.

Make handling finances fun and pleasurable. Whenever you sit down for a money management session, light candles and/or play music that pleases you. Grab a hot cup of Chai and relax. Make it an act of hygge! As you associate handling money with pleasure and not pain, you start enjoying the process and having fun. You become more cognizant of your irrelevant expenses and stop making stupid choices. You realize that you are in better control of your finances when you change the way you feel about money. It brings a revolution both to your mindset and your account balance.

In essence, it's all about making choices that serve you well and nurturing a loving relationship with the money that comes into your life.

Day 14: Become a Badass

"By embracing money and getting into the flow, you open yourself up to the abundance that is trying to reach you at this very moment."
— Jen Sincero, *You Are a Badass at Making Money*

If you want to become rich and bring the amount of money you desire in your life, what service are you willing to provide in exchange? What's your plan and most importantly what's holding you back? You need to take charge of your thoughts and actions and set yourself up for financial success. As Jordan Belfort rightly says: "The only thing standing between you and your goal is the bullshit story you keep telling yourself as to why you can't achieve it." Be careful about who you surround yourself with, as they can influence your thoughts in a big way.

As we grow, we start accruing various limiting beliefs around money. Dissect them and become aware of your worries and fears. Envision your ideal life and your most authentic self. What is that person about and what role money plays in his or her life? You have to find out what being rich means to you.

Only then, you'll be truly inspired to become wealthy. Strive to become the badass you know you are and start accruing the wealth you know you deserve.

Once you're fired up and have an action plan in place, it's time to let go of all fears and dive all in. Sometimes you need to start running before you can walk. Don't let anything sway your determination to transform this aspect of your life. Believe in yourself and the service you provide and have faith that the Universe is bringing your desired wealth to you.

Day 15: Automate Your Finances

"How much you earn has almost no bearing on whether or not you can and will build wealth. Regardless of the size of your paycheck, you probably already make enough money to become rich."
— David Bach, *The Automatic Millionaire*

Many times we spend money half-consciously on trivial things, whether it be our morning coffee, having lunch outside or buying unnecessary stuff on Amazon. These may seem innocuous expenses, but they add up and cost us a lot in the long term. They're like those thousand small cuts that kill our future financial well-being.

If you're someone who is struggling with managing finances and making payments on time, there's an easier and effortless way to be on top of all of it. All you have to do is simply switch from this impulsive autopilot mode to a more deliberate and conscious one that supports your financial growth. This can be achieved by automation. Whatever your current goal is right now, whether it be saving, investing or paying off your debt, make it automatic. This will free up your time as well as the energy that you spend in igniting your willpower. We are blessed that we have the privilege of automating our finances online with minimal effort.

Make paying yourself first a priority. When you automate it, this is already taken care of before your paycheck amount gets deposited in your bank. You magically start to live below your means. Humans are incredible at adapting when we need to. If you leave the savings and investments to manage yourself, it requires a lot of discipline and resilience. But when you automate them, it's much easier and with zero worries. It frees up your mental faculties which can be used for other higher purposes.

Day 16: Think Long-Term

"One dollar invested today can easily be worth $15 in forty years; but if you wait ten more years to get started, the same dollar might only grow to $7.50. Imagine how different your lifestyle would be in your later years with twice the amount of money in the bank."

— Patrick O'Shaughnessy, *Millennial Money*

If you are a millennial then there's a high chance that keeping money aside for retirement is not a priority for you. But if you do it, you have a major advantage because time is on your side. If you're someone who believes in saving money, you're on the right track, but you need to tweak your approach. Saving is fine, but if you really want to see your money grow, the best way to get ahead in the game is to invest it. In the long-term, your money loses value because of low interest rates in a savings account. But when you invest your money in the stock market, you get higher gains overall.

The average life expectancy has increased tremendously. And it's wise to not rely on the government for any benefits after the retirement age. The best plan is to be self-reliant and invest your money in stocks. Diversify your money across different markets and countries. As international currencies change in value differently from the one in your own country, you may set yourself up for huge returns. Think out of the box when you invest and don't go with the herd. Do your research and make choices that are profitable. Look for the best bargains that you can find, and understand when a particular stock is riding a wave of momentum. When you invest at the right time, you maximize your future returns.

Control your fears, impulses and greediness and think of the bigger picture. Avoiding instant gratification will serve you well.

Day 17: Become Unshakeable

"You need to learn the rules of the financial game, who the players are, what their agendas are, where you can get hurt, and how you can win. This knowledge can set you free."
— Anthony Robbins, *Unshakeable: Your Financial Freedom Playbook*

The money game is not only about surviving but also about thriving. Saving and investing can be two things that you can do right now for the betterment of the future you. Compound interest is magical. If you can invest even a small amount of money every month, day by day it'll keep growing and you don't have to worry about it. The sooner you start, the more your money will grow.

We have to study the patterns of the financial market and distinguish a good investment from the bad one. It is wise for us to educate ourselves with regard to how we can protect the downside and minimize the risks. The higher risk and reward equation does not hold true for the stock market. To become a good investor we have to master the art of asymmetric risk/reward. We need to seek investments that are low risk and offer us high rewards. Along with that, being aware of the taxes and fees that we will encounter makes us better and smarter investors.

Even the experts and the superstars of the stock market don't know what the future holds. So, beware of the gurus and the pundits who claim to know all the secrets of how it works.

As an antidote to the unpredictability of the stock market, diversify your portfolio. Feel free to explore as this can be done across different asset classes, countries and currencies over time.

Day 18: Raise Your Financial IQ

"The best way to measure your investing success is not by whether you're beating the market but by whether you've put in place a financial plan and a behavioral discipline that are likely to get you where you want to go."

— Benjamin Graham, *The Intelligent Investor*

I magine the stock market as a person who is gullible, highly susceptible to other people's influence and has unpredictable mood swings. You know trusting this person can have dangerous consequences. The best way to invest is to never react to what this person is doing and make intelligent moves.

Success in the stock market can only be measured by long-term analysis. Intelligent investors research well and only invest when they know that they can have safe and steady returns. They don't follow trends but rather only invest when the pricing is below the intrinsic value.

Intelligent investors only care about making a profit for themselves and don't worry about outperforming others or staying ahead of the competition. They're good at avoiding temptations and greed, as they don't believe in fast money, but in getting rich slowly.

The easiest way to invest without risks is to study the investment funds that have had long-term success and model them. Automate your investments every month so that you're investing a fixed amount no matter what. This will cultivate discipline as well as make you emotionally strong when you get tempted to invest more.

Continual research and monitoring of portfolios will make the profit flow coming. If you're a beginner, a great strategy would be to make online investments and study the different investment options. In this way, you will train yourself to find bargains and learn the inner workings of the stock market. Your goal is to make investments that generate gradual and steady profits.

Day 19: Embrace Nobility

"Take out a dollar bill and look at it. Now pat yourself on your back because you are looking at a certificate of performance."
— Daniel Lapin, *Thou Shall Prosper*

The Torah, the holy book that defines Jewish law, refers to business as a noble pursuit and hence earning money as an honest and genuine endeavor to better lives. According to the Jewish tradition, businesses should not be driven by greed or any other negative emotion, but it's also important to sustain themselves so they can continue helping others.

They believe money is an entity that strengthens the bond between people. It symbolizes trust when it flows from one person to another during a transaction. Money is something that needs to keep moving between people and is not to be hidden. The more active your money is, the more prosperity you will have.

The Jewish emphasize giving away money for charitable causes as the most effective way to increase your income. The giver is always at a spiritual advantage as compared to the receiver. And people are more inspired to do business with the person who is established as a giver.

The Jewish also believe that there is nothing called retirement because when you retire, you stop adding value to others. In fact, it's better to continue working as you grow old because you're more in touch with your spirituality and have a wealth of experience to share. You can offer guidance to others and earn money in exchange. Also, as you grow old, you gather more connections; and hence your earning potential keeps growing as well. Life is all about the journey and not the destination, and hence you should never stop earning money.

Day 20: Money vs. Life

"Money is something we choose to trade our life energy for."
— Vicki Robin, *Your Money or Your Life*

Does your current work and lifestyle reflect your most important values? In reality, most people work so that they can earn money, not because they love doing it. They lack the need for self-actualization and direction in their lives.

We all work 40+ hour work weeks in order to have enough money to enjoy life and spend on material possessions and luxury. On the contrary, it would be wise to buy less so that we can save and invest enough money to retire early. We trade our precious time for money so that we can live a life of luxury and buy stuff. If this transaction feels meaningless and shallow to you, then maybe it's best you start thinking about the alternative option: degrading your lifestyle, reducing your living expenses, finding ways to increase your income, and investing the difference. This will serve you in quitting your boring job and retiring early.

Track your income and all your expenses. Work on widening the gap between the income that you make and your total expenses, and invest the difference. Once the income from your investments is greater than your living expenses, you reach a significant point. Here, you're free to quit your job if you like and live the way you want to live.

It's not much about money, but rather about the relationship that you have with money. And the best way to improve your life and your relationship with money is to align yourself with your core values.

Day 21: Being Honest and Ethical

"As I've come to discover, investing is about much more than money. So as your wealth grows, I hope you will also come to realize that the money is largely irrelevant. And what you will want to do with the bulk of your wealth is give it back to society."
— Guy Spier, *The Education of a Value Investor*

An elite education from a business school or university is not very effective. They teach us how to solve problems based on theories rather than teaching the skills necessary to solve real-world problems. The harsh truth is that jobs in the real world may force you to go against your core values and ethics. Other people's actions and difficult circumstances may tempt you to choose the easy way out by manipulating people, instead of using honest methods to gain business. We need to understand that these past mistakes don't define us and we can start with a blank slate if we choose to!

The value investing philosophy teaches you to have unwavering faith in your investments, and focus on the bigger picture. The risk is minimal and the ethics are sound, hence a double advantage! Because this is a long-term process, positive thinking will take you far; your attitude determines your altitude. Developing emotional intelligence, discipline and prioritizing ethics over profit will make you much happier and fulfilled.

We need to build credibility and trust with the people we work with. Being genuine, honest and helpful will spark people's interest in you and your business. When we focus on giving without selfish gains and building relationships, we attract success, wealth, and prosperity. With value investing, the goal is to not only become a better investor, but also a better person.

Pithy Insights

- *The more you give, the more you'll get.*
- *Pay yourself first.*
- *Formal education is not enough; to become a millionaire you need to become a lifelong learner.*
- *Don't work hard for money, let money work hard for you.*
- *Avoid instant gratification and focus on long-term wins.*
- *Paying off your credit card debt and other loans first is the best investment you can make for your future.*
- *Get disciplined and organized.*
- *Automation will make personal finances management easier and effortless.*
- *Start investing early so that both time and the magic of compound interest are on your side.*
- *Develop a loving relationship with your money.*
- *Track your income and expenses.*
- *Embrace minimalism and focus on saving and investing your money.*
- *Strive to become an entrepreneur, not an employee, if you want to become wealthy.*
- *Getting rich is a slow and steady process.*
- *Diversify your investments across different asset classes, countries and currencies.*
- *Look for the best bargains and invest at the right time so that*

you maximize your future gains.

- *Focus on building relationships and trust; not on earning money.*
- *Take calculated risks and always protect your downside.*
- *Invest intelligently and don't worry about the competition or outperforming others.*
- *Build trust and credibility in your professional relationships, and always make money through honest and ethical means. Prioritize ethics over profits.*
- *Don't give in to fear, greed and other negative emotions, and invest consistently.*
- *Monitor your habits and avoid self-sabotaging behaviors.*
- *When you accumulate debt, you rob your future self's money, happiness, and well-being.*
- *Growth and expansion is the way of nature. Hence, it is natural for you to become rich and wealthy. It's your birthright!*
- *Managing finances is an act of self-care.*
- *Make a life-long commitment to financial education.*
- *The stock market is unpredictable; never trust any financial guru who claims to know how things are going to turn out.*
- *Live a simple life and spend less than what you make.*
- *Always remember, the borrower becomes a slave to the lender. Become a lender, not a borrower!*
- *True wealth is not only about making money but also about having great health and high-quality relationships.*
- *Becoming rich is the best way to inspire others.*
- *Make visualization of your abundant future a daily practice.*
- *Believe before you see; manifestations take some time to gestate and come into physical reality.*
- *Make managing personal finances a fun and pleasurable process, not a painful one.*
- *Have an unwavering faith in yourself.*

- *Design a road map that will take you from where you are to where you want to be.*
- *Have a written plan and budget to make the most out of the money that comes your way.*
- *Associate exclusively with people who are wealthy and challenge you to grow; your associations determine your wealth.*
- *Get rid of all your limiting beliefs and strive to become your ideal self.*
- *Do the work that you love and fulfills your need for meaning, joy, and money.*
- *When you focus on adding value to other people's lives, you attract success and wealth.*
- *The giver is always at a spiritual advantage when compared to the receiver.*

References and Suggestions for Further Reading

In addition to the exceptional books mentioned previously in the daily meditations, there are a handful of recent works by some amazing authors and thought leaders that you should most definitely read to develop a wealth mindset. Here is a comprehensive list of all the best resources on finances, money management, and investing for you:

Bach, D. (2006). *Start Late, Finish Rich: A No-Fail Plan for Achieving Financial Freedom at Any Age* (Reprint ed.). Currency.

Bach, D. (2016). *The Automatic Millionaire, Expanded and Updated: A Powerful One-Step Plan to Live and Finish Rich* (Expanded, Updated ed.). Crown.

Bach, D. (2018). *Smart Women Finish Rich, Expanded and Updated* (Expanded, Updated ed.). Currency.

Bach, D., & Mann, J. D. (2019). *The Latte Factor: Why You Don't Have to Be Rich to Live Rich* (Illustrated ed.). Atria Books.

Bogle, J. C. (2017). *The Little Book of Common Sense Investing: The Only Way to Guarantee Your Fair Share of Stock Market Returns (Little Books, Big Profits)* (Updated and Revised ed.). Wiley.

Clason, G. S. (2018). *The Richest Man In Babylon - Original Edition* (Original ed.). Dauphin Publications Inc.

Cruze, R. (2016). *Love Your Life Not Theirs: 7 Money Habits for Living the Life You Want* (1st ed.). Ramsey Press.

Cruze, R., & Ramsey, D. (2021). *Know Yourself, Know Your Money: Discover WHY you handle money the way you do, and WHAT to do about it!* Ramsey Press.

DeMarco, M. J. (2011). *The Millionaire Fastlane: Crack the Code to Wealth and Live Rich for a Lifetime* (1st ed.). Viperion Publishing Corporation.

Eker, H. T. (2007). *Secrets of the Millionaire Mind*. Harper.

Graham, B., Zweig, J., & Buffett, W. E. (2006). *The Intelligent Investor: The Definitive Book on Value Investing. A Book of Practical Counsel (Revised Edition)* (Revised ed.). Harper Business.

Hicks, E., & Hicks, J. (2019). *Money, and the Law of Attraction: Learning to Attract Wealth, Health, and Happiness.* Hay House Inc.

Hill, N. (2016). *Think and Grow Rich (An Official Publication of the Napoleon Hill Foundation)* (Original First Edition 1937 ed.). Sound Wisdom.

Hill, N., & Pell, A. (2005). *Think and Grow Rich: The Landmark Bestseller—Now Revised and Updated for the 21st Century* (Rev Exp ed.). Tarcher.

Hogan, C., & Ramsey, D. (2016). *Retire Inspired: It's Not an Age, It's a Financial Number* (1st ed.). Ramsey Press.

Hogan, C., & Ramsey, D. (2019). *Everyday Millionaires.* Ramsey Press.

Honda, K. (2020). *Happy Money.* Hodder And Stoughton Limited.

Housel, M. (2020). *The Psychology of Money: Timeless lessons on wealth, greed, and happiness.* Harriman House.

Kiyosaki, R. T. (2015). *Rich Dad's CASHFLOW Quadrant: Rich Dad's Guide to Financial Freedom.* Plata Publishing.

Kiyosaki, R. T. (2017). *Rich Dad Poor Dad: What the Rich Teach Their Kids About Money That the Poor and Middle Class Do Not!* (Second ed.). Plata Publishing.

Lapin, R. D. (2009). *Thou Shall Prosper: Ten Commandments for Making Money* (2nd ed.). Wiley.

Northrup, K. (2013). *Money, A Love Story: Untangle Your Financial Woes and Create the Life You Really Want*. Hay House Inc.

ONeal, A., & Ramsey, D. (2019). *Debt Free Degree*. Ramsey Press.

O'Shaughnessy, P. (2014). *Millennial Money: How Young Investors Can Build a Fortune*. St. Martin's Press.

Ramsey, D. (2013). *The Total Money Makeover: Classic Edition: A Proven Plan for Financial Fitness* (1st ed.). Thomas Nelson.

Ramsey, D. (2021). *Dave Ramsey's Complete Guide To Money* (1st ed.). Ramsey Press.

Ramsey, D., & Cruze, R. (2014). *Smart Money Smart Kids: Raising the Next Generation to Win with Money* (1st ed.). Ramsey Press.

Richards, C. C. R. (2021). *The One-Page Financial Plan*. Penguin Books Ltd.

Robbins, T. (2016). *MONEY Master the Game: 7 Simple Steps to Financial Freedom* (Updated ed.). Simon & Schuster.

Robbins, T., & Mallouk, P. (2018). *Unshakeable: Your Financial Freedom Playbook* (Reprint ed.). Simon & Schuster.

Robin, V., Dominguez, J., & Mustache, M. (2008). *Your Money or Your Life: 9 Steps to Transforming Your Relationship with Money and Achieving Financial Independence: Fully Revised and Updated for 2018* (Revised ed.). Penguin Books.

Sethi, R. (2009). *I Will Teach You To Be Rich* (1st ed.). Workman Publishing.

Sethi, R. (2019). *I Will Teach You to Be Rich, Second Edition: No Guilt. No Excuses. No BS. Just a 6-Week Program That Works* (Revised ed.). Workman Publishing Company.

Sincero, J. (2018). *You Are a Badass at Making Money: Master the Mindset of Wealth* (Reprint ed.). Penguin Life.

Spier, G. (2014). *The Education of a Value Investor: My Transformative Quest for Wealth, Wisdom, and Enlightenment.* St. Martin's Press.

Stanley, T. J. (2001). *The Millionaire Mind* (Illustrated ed.). Andrews McMeel Publishing.

Stanley, T. J., & Danko, W. D. (2010). *The Millionaire Next Door: The Surprising Secrets of America's Wealthy* (Reissue ed.). Taylor Trade Publishing.

Wattles, W. D. (2007). *The Science of Getting Rich* (0 ed.). Tarcher/Penguin.

If you think this book has added value to you and helped you in any way, please consider giving a copy to your loved ones, family members, coworkers, friends or someone you just met, whom you care about and want greater success for. When we help others and give away our time, earnings, and most importantly our heart, the ripple effect ends up bringing more abundance and prosperity to us.

To read more essays on how to create an extraordinary life and become a better version of yourself every day, please visit my website: ParthSawhney.com

Parth Sawhney is an author and success mentor to high-achievers all around the world. Through his writing and other meaningful creations, Parth shares life-changing ideas, insights and resources related to personal development, philosophy, success psychology and the human condition. His recent books include *The Daily Apple*, *Thriving in the New Normal*, *The Way of the Karma Yogi*, and *The Detachment Manifesto*. When he is not working, Parth enjoys spending time in coffee shops and taking long walks.

www.ingramcontent.com/pod-product-compliance
Lightning Source LLC
Chambersburg PA
CBHW021351160726
47994CB00007B/2909